A Character Building Book™

Learning About Integrity from the Life of
Eleanor Roosevelt

Nancy Ellwood

The Rosen Publishing Group's
PowerKids Press™
New York

For my mom, Nancy P. Ellwood, the most extraordinary person I'll ever know.

Published in 1999 by The Rosen Publishing Group, Inc.
29 East 21st Street, New York, NY 10010

First Edition

Book Design: Erin McKenna

Photo Credits: pp. 4, 7, 8, 11, 19 © Franklin D. Roosevelt Library/Corbis-Bettmann; p. 12 © The National Archives/Corbis Bettmann; p. 15 © UPI/Corbis-Bettmann; p. 16 © Library of Congress/Corbis-Bettmann; p. 20 © Hulton-Deutsch Collection/Corbis-Bettmann.

Ellwood, Nancy.
    Learning about integrity from the life of Eleanor Roosevelt/ by Nancy Ellwood.
        p.   cm. — (A character building book)
    Includes index.
    Summary: A brief biography examining the value of integrity in the life of the First Lady who devoted herself to helping others and working for peace.
    ISBN 0-8239-5316-0
    1. Roosevelt, Eleanor, 1884–1962—Juvenile literature. 2. Presidents' spouses—United States—Biography—Juvenile literature. 3. Integrity—Juvenile literature. [1. Roosevelt, Eleanor, 1884–1962. 2. First ladies. 3. Women—Biography. 4. Integrity.] I. Title. II. Series.
    E807.1.R48E45 1998
    973.917′092—dc21
    [B]   98-21929
                                                                               CIP
                                                                                AC

Manufactured in the United States of America

Contents

Helping the Nation

Eleanor Roosevelt is one of the most admired women of the 20th century. As a young woman and then as wife of President Franklin Delano Roosevelt, or FDR, Eleanor worked hard to help poor women and children around the nation. Even after FDR's death in 1945, Eleanor was still an important person to the people of the United States. She fought for **civil rights** (SIH-vul RYTS), women's rights, and world peace. Eleanor always stood up for what she believed in with strength and **integrity** (in-TEH-grih-tee).

◄ *Eleanor will always be known as one of the most important people in the fight for fairness around the world.*

Growing Up

Anna Eleanor Roosevelt was born on October 11, 1884 in New York City. She was a quiet little girl. When Eleanor was eight years old her mother died. Eleanor and her brothers went to live with their grandparents. Eleanor missed her mother and was sad to leave her father. But her father wrote her many letters. In these letters he told Eleanor to be strong and to study hard in school. That's exactly what she did. Then, when she was ten, Eleanor's father died. This made her even more lonely.

Eleanor kept the letters that her father had written her when she was a little girl. She carried them with her for the rest of her life. ▶

Learning Integrity

When Eleanor was fifteen, she went to school in England. She was shy and **insecure** (in-seh-KYUR). But at school Eleanor became close to a teacher named Ms. Souvestre. Ms. Souvestre made Eleanor speak up in class and say what she truly felt. This helped Eleanor build **confidence** (KON-fih-dents). Ms. Souvestre was helping Eleanor realize that she was smart. She taught Eleanor to always stand up for what she believed, no matter who **challenged** (CHA-lenjd) her. Eleanor first learned about integrity from Ms. Souvestre.

◀ *This photo of Eleanor was taken the summer before she went to the Allenswood School in England. She was fourteen years old.*

Eleanor and FDR

In 1905 Eleanor married Franklin Delano Roosevelt. At that time, FDR was a young man studying to be a lawyer. Because FDR loved law and the government, he decided that he wanted to get involved in **politics** (POL-ih-tiks). Unlike many men at the time, FDR talked with his wife about his job and the decisions he had to make. And unlike many women, Eleanor wanted to learn about politics and the government.

Unlike many women of her time, Eleanor spoke with FDR and his business partners about government and politics. ▶

A Turning Point

By 1918 FDR had become a well-known politician. But Eleanor was bored with only learning about politics. She wanted to do more. During this time, the United States was fighting in World War I. So Eleanor **volunteered** (vah-lun-TEERD) for the Red Cross. She helped collect and send warm clothes to soldiers who were fighting in Europe. She visited sick soldiers in hospitals. After the war ended, Eleanor and FDR traveled to Europe. They saw the **destruction** (dih-STRUK-shun) caused by war.

◀ *Eleanor was deeply affected by the soldiers she met and the damage she saw in Europe after World War I.*

Eleanor the Activist

In 1921 FDR caught a terrible disease called polio. It left him **paralyzed** (PA-rih-lyzd). While FDR tried to get better, Eleanor got more involved in programs in New York City. Women had just won the right to vote, but they still didn't have many of the rights that men had. So Eleanor became an **activist** (AK-tih-vist) for women's rights. She joined the League of Women Voters and **encouraged** (en-KUR-ijd) women to fight for their rights. Eleanor also wrote articles and spoke on radio shows and at colleges.

Eleanor became very well known because of her work helping those in need. ▶

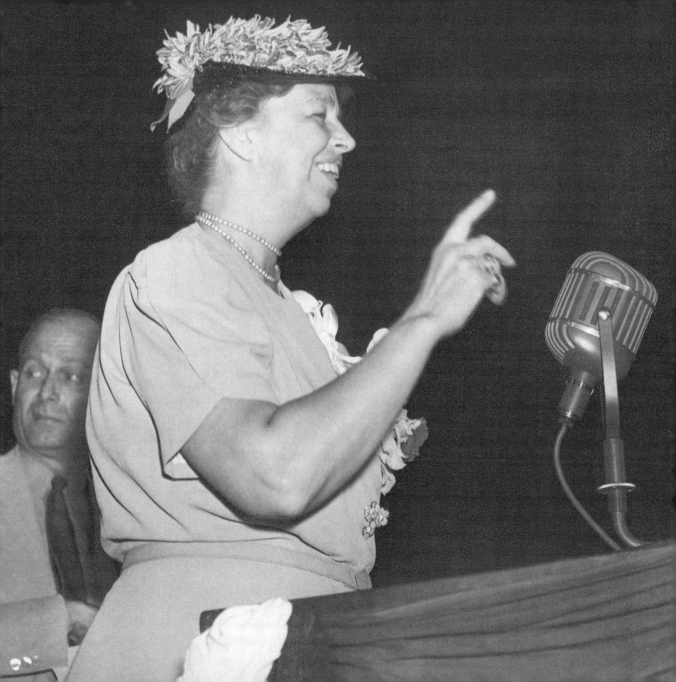

Working Hard

Throughout the 1920s, Eleanor became more and more active. She fought for the rights of children who were forced to work instead of being allowed to go to school. She fought for the rights of men, women, and children who worked long hours in dangerous factories. She also taught at a girls' school. Many people got angry at Eleanor for speaking up and trying to change things. But Eleanor didn't care. She knew what she was doing was right. She showed the world she would always stand up for people who needed help.

Eleanor loved to teach. She taught young women about the things she felt were most important: history, government, and the importance of learning.

First Lady

In 1932 FDR was elected president. The country was suffering from the **Great Depression** (GRAYT de-PREH-shun). Many people had no jobs or money. FDR set up **relief** (ree-LEEF) programs to help these people. As First Lady, Eleanor traveled around the country to talk to the American people about the programs. She learned that African Americans were not allowed to work in the programs. Eleanor was angry about this. So she helped get laws passed that allowed them to work in the relief programs.

As First Lady, Eleanor would talk only to female reporters. This forced newspapers around the country to hire women reporters for the first time. ▶

On Her Own

FDR died in 1945. A new president took office, and Eleanor thought that her job was done. But she was wrong.

Organizations around the country wanted Eleanor to speak at their events. She kept giving speeches and writing articles and books. She was the first woman ever to have her own national newspaper column, which was called "My Day." Eleanor was also the first woman to have her own radio show. The whole world listened to what Eleanor had to say.

◀ *From 1945 until 1962, Eleanor often spoke and wrote about world peace.*

A Woman of Integrity

Until her death in 1962, Eleanor continued to fight for the rights of women and **minorities** (my-NOR-ih-teez). She worked with the United Nations to help write and pass laws that made sure people around the world were treated fairly. No matter who fought against her, Eleanor always fought back. Her life has **inspired** (in-SPYRD) men and women to stand up for their rights and the rights of others.

Eleanor Roosevelt is still respected today by people everywhere because of her fairness and integrity.

Glossary

activist (AK-tih-vist) A person who fights for what she believes.

challenge (CHA-lenj) To fight against.

civil rights (SIH-vul RYTS) The rights of citizens regardless of their race, age, religion, or sex.

confidence (KON-fih-dents) Believing in yourself.

destruction (dih-STRUK-shun) Great damage or ruin.

encourage (en-KUR-ij) Give support to.

Great Depression (GRAYT de-PREH-shun) A time in the 1930s when banks and businesses lost money, causing many people to lose their jobs.

insecure (in-seh-KYUR) Not feeling good about yourself.

inspire (in-SPYR) To fill with excitement about something.

integrity (in-TEH-grih-tee) The firm support of ideas that you believe in.

minority (my-NOR-ih-tee) A group of people that is in some way different from other people around them.

paralyzed (PA-rih-lyzd) When you can't feel or move your body.

politics (POL-ih-tiks) Having to do with elections and governments.

relief (ree-LEEF) Help for those who need it.

volunteer (vah-lun-TEER) To dedicate your time to a cause without being paid.

Index